First Principles and Follow Up Studies

Dr. Kip McKean

All proceeds from this book go directly to the McKean Scholarship Foundation of MERCY*worldwide*. The McKean Scholarship Foundation was established in 2020 by Dr. Kip McKean in honor of his parents Admiral & Mrs. Thomas W. and Kim McKean. These funds are used exclusively to support educational opportunities for third world children.

FIRST PRINCIPLES AND FOLLOW UP STUDIES

Cover Credit of Bible Codex – Jake Studer

ISBN: 9798680392805

First Print – Sixth Edition

TABLE OF CONTENTS

FIRST PRINCIPLES AND FOLLOW UP STUDIES

"For although by this time you should be teachers, you... need to have someone teach you the rudiments of the first principles of the revelations of God... Therefore leaving the teaching of the first principles of Christ, let's press on to perfection – not laying again a foundation... of faith toward God, of the teaching of baptisms, of laying on of hands, of resurrection of the dead and of eternal judgment. This will we do." **Hebrews 5:12; 6:1-3 (WEB)**

Originally, the *First Principle Studies* were compiled and published in 1980, while I served the Lord during the formative early days of the Boston Church of Christ. In fact, the building of these studies was a process. *The Baptism Of The Holy Spirit* and *The Miraculous Gifts Of The Holy Spirit Studies* were my "gleanings" from The Acts Class at the 14th Street Church of Christ in Gainesville, Florida in 1973. *The Seeking God, The Word Of God, Light And Darkness, New Testament Conversion,* and *The Church Studies* were written in 1976-1977 when the Spirit initiated the Eastern Illinois University Campus Ministry in Charleston, Illinois. *The Coming Of The Kingdom Study* was penned after I completed The Old Testament Survey Class at Harding Graduate School of Religion in Memphis, Tennessee in the summer of 1978. The *Discipleship Study* was originally written while I was reaching out to a religious student at Harvard University in Cambridge, Massachusetts in February 1980. (*The Cross Study* was formally added in 1982.)

It was at this point in early 1980 that I pulled these studies together calling them the *First Principles.* For the conclusion of each session of teaching *First Principles,* I would preach a four-part overview of the Book of Acts for my students to have a shared vision for the evangelization of the nations. Tests and quizzes were administered covering each *First Principle Study,* that week's memory work, the order of the books of the Bible, and in the later weeks, the Book of Acts.

The first four *Follow Up Studies* were written in 1988 to help mature the almost 1,500 "baby Christians" baptized that year in the Boston Church of Christ. The *Persecution Study* was authored in Portland, Oregon in 2005 while we were undergoing heavy persecution by the world and even by those who called themselves "Christians."

The *First Principles* were slightly revised in 2003 to meet the needs and to confront the challenges of the Portland International Church of Christ. While planting and leading the City of Angels International Christian Church in Los Angeles, I made a few more modifications in 2007 and 2012. As well, after spending considerable time on the international mission field, I further adapted the studies in 2018 and 2020. As of today, these essentially same *First Principles Studies* from 1980 are being taught to all of the new disciples in the over 100 International Christian Churches in 47 nations in their local languages. May the Lord continue to "solidify, unify and multiply" sold-out disciples everywhere for the evangelization of all the nations in this generation! And to God be all the glory!

Dr. Kip McKean
August 8, 2020

COURSE INFORMATION

1. This course should take a high priority in your day as it is geared to help you grasp a firmer hold on God's Word and to deepen your understanding of His will for your life.

2. Each session two new Scriptures should be memorized for a written or verbal quiz at the beginning of each class.

3. Each study's content and the order of Scriptures should also be memorized for the quiz.

4. Each student is required to memorize the names of all the books of the Bible.

5. Read Ron Harding's *The Untold Story: Chronicles Of Modern-Day Christianity* by Session 8.

6. An outline of the Book of Acts will be turned in by session 11. Each student is required to memorize two points from each chapter in the Book of Acts.

OUTLINE OF CLASSES

Session 1	Introduction And Seeking God
Session 2	The Word Of God
Session 3	Discipleship
Session 4	The Coming Of The Kingdom
Session 5	Light And Darkness
Session 6	New Testament Conversion
Session 7	The Cross
Session 8	The Baptism With The Holy Spirit
Session 9	The Miraculous Gifts Of The Holy Spirit
Session 10	The Church
Sessions 11-14	The Book Of Acts

SUGGESTED READING LIST

These books are recommended as thought-provoking and informative tools to be used in gaining insights into God's Word. Some of the books are not Biblically correct on all doctrinal points.

Chapman: *The Five Love Languages*
Coleman: *The Master Plan Of Evangelism*
Edwards: *The Tale Of Three Kings*
McKean: *Elevate – Jesus' Global Revolution For Women*
Moreno: *A Battle That Even Kings Lost*
Rivers: *Voice In The Wind*
Smellie: *Proven Genuine – An Examination Of Suffering In The Book Of Job*
Taylor: *The Disciplined Life*

SCRIPTURE MEMORY

"But in your hearts set apart Christ as Lord. Always be prepared to give an answer to everyone who asks you to give the reason for the hope that you have. But do this with gentleness and respect." 1 Peter 3:15

Session 1	Session 2	Session 3
Jeremiah 29:11	John 8:31-32	Mark 1:17
Matthew 6:33	Philippians 4:13	John 13:34-35

Session 4	Session 5	Session 6
Acts 2:38	Ezekiel 18:20	Matthew 22:37-39
Philippians 4:4	Galatians 1:8	John 15:8

Session 7	Session 8	Session 9
Matthew 28:18-20	Hebrews 10:23-25	Hebrews 12:15
Luke 19:10	1 John 1:9	Hebrews 13:17

INTRODUCTION TO THE COURSE

1. Course Requirements
2. Purpose of First Principles Class
   A. Solidify – Hebrews 5:11-14; 6:1-3
   B. Unify – John 13:34-35
   C. Multiply – Matthew 28:18-20
3. How to win people to Christ
   A. Build a good friendship
      i. Spend time
      ii. Have discussions
   B. Find out their background
      i. Life story (also share yours)
      ii. Present beliefs about God, Christ and the Bible
   C. Ask your friend to study the Bible with you.
   D. Buy a Bible as a gift
      i. A readable version
      ii. Inscribe a meaningful thought
   E. If they are an unbeliever about Jesus or if they are unclear about Him then…
      i. Study the Book of John or *The Jesus Study Series.*
      ii. Purpose **(John 20:30-31)**
   F. If they believe in Jesus start with the *Seeking God Study.*
4. **Have a Christian friend you are discipling in on the study as well. Take concise notes for your non-Christian friend, so they can go back and review what has been studied.**

SEEKING GOD

1. **Psalm 119:1-2**
   A. Blessed means happy (superlatively happy)
   B. Happiness is not the goal of one who seeks God but the "by-product."
   C. To seek God, you must do it with all your heart.
   D. Seeking God means to "keep His statutes."

2. **Matthew 6:25-34**
   A. Do not worry – ironic – cannot add a single hour to your life.
   B. God knows your needs.
   C. Seek first His kingdom and righteousness...
   D. Then God will give you everything you need.

3. **Acts 17:26-28**
   A. God determines the times and places each person lives.
   B. He does this so man will seek Him, reach out for Him, and find Him.
   C. God is not far from anyone.
   D. A Christian meeting you is not by chance – but of God.

4. **John 4:23-24**
   A. God seeks men...
   B. Men who want to worship Him in spirit and in truth

5. **Acts 17:10-12**
   A. Read and study the Bible for your own convictions.
   B. Read and study the Bible daily.

6. **Jeremiah 29:11-14**
   A. God has an individual plan for your life.
   B. A plan to prosper you – with hope and a future.
   C. You will find God when you seek Him with all your heart.

7. **Acts 8:26-39**

   A. The angels and the Holy Spirit are helping you to get to God.

   B. Do not be afraid to ask questions about life or the Bible – be humble.

   C. You need someone to explain the Bible to you.

   D. You will be "rejoicing" when you find God.

8. **Matthew 7:7-8**

   A. Seek and God guarantees you will find Him.

   B. Ask God for help.

THE WORD OF GOD

1. **2 Timothy 3:16-17**
   A. All Scripture is inspired by God.
   B. It is to be applied to our lives.

2. **Hebrews 4:12-13**
   A. The Word is relevant.
   B. The Word cuts (hurts) – compare it to a scalpel.
   C. It is good to be cut because it cuts the "cancer" (sin) out.

3. **2 Peter 1: 20-21**
   A. There is no private interpretation of the Bible.
   B. The Holy Spirit inspired the men who wrote the books of the Bible.

4. **John 8:31-32**
   A. Intellectual belief is not enough – nor can we go by our feelings.
   B. A person must hold on to and follow the teachings of Jesus to be a true disciple.
   C. Sincerity does not equal truth.
   D. Religious people can be wrong.

5. **Matthew 15:1-9**
   A. Do not go by traditions or creeds.
   B. Worship by traditions (which supersede the Word of God) is worship in vain.

6. **1 Timothy 4:16**
   A. Watch your life and doctrine closely – they are inseparable.
   B. Which is more important, life or doctrine? Both: An airplane with only one wing cannot fly.
   C. Why is it so important to learn and to teach and to live the right doctrine? To save yourself and those who hear you.

7. **Acts 17:10-12**
   A. Must check what religious leaders say.
   B. Your challenge: Read and study the Bible every day.

8. **James 1:22-25**
   A. The Word of God is a mirror.
   B. Do not forget what you see – "do what it says."

9. **John 12:48**
   A. Why study the Bible? The Word will judge us.
   B. Decision: Will I live by the Bible or my feelings, traditions, needs, etc.?

DISCIPLESHIP

Introduction: Matthew 28:18-20

    A. What does Jesus want everybody to become?

    B. Which is the more popular term – "Disciple" or "Christian?" The word "Christian" only appears 3 times in the New Testament. It is the name those in the world gave the disciples, seven years after the church began. (**Acts 11:19-26**) The word "Disciple" occurs over 270 times in the New Testament.

    C. SAVED = CHRISTIAN = DISCIPLE

    D. Jesus came to make disciples. Only baptized disciples will be saved.

Jesus defines disciple, thus defining who is a true Christian.

1. Mark 1:14-18

    A. This was the calling of the first disciples.

    B. Jesus said, "Come follow me."

    C. "Fishers of men" – Jesus gave these first disciples the real purpose for living.

    D. Immediately, they followed Him.

2. Luke 9:23-26

    A. "If any man" means everyone… and anyone (v. 23).

    B. "Deny self" is to be like Christ in the Garden recorded in **Matthew 26:36-39**, "Not my will, but your will." Do not give into moods, emotions, etc.

    C. "Carry the cross daily." Die to ourselves every day (v. 23).

    D. Either gain world and forfeit your soul or lose your life for Jesus and save it (v. 25).

3. Luke 14:25-33

    A. "If any man" means everyone… and anyone (v. 26).

    B. Count the cost (v. 28-30)

C. Consider the alternatives (v. 31-32)
D. Love Christ more than any person (v. 26)
E. Persecutions (v. 27)
F. Everything means everything (v. 33)

4. Luke 11:1-4
    A. Must learn to pray. The disciples saw the strength Jesus received from the Father.
    B. A daily personal relationship with God will have daily prayers (v. 3).

5. John 13:34-35
    A. Love one another.
    B. Be an active part of the fellowship.

6. Matthew 28:18-20
    A. The command – "make disciples" – is given to all.
    B. Who is a candidate for baptism? People who make the decision to be a disciple.
    C. You need someone to disciple you to maturity in Christ.
    D. This is the only way to save the world!

Year	Preacher	Disciple
1	365	2
2	730	4
3	1095	8
13	4745	8192
33	12,045	the world, 8 billion plus

Conclusion Questions: Am I a disciple? Am I a Christian? Am I saved? What do I need to do to become a disciple?

17

THE COMING OF THE KINGDOM

In this study you will see the continuity of the Old and New Testaments.

Questions: What is the Kingdom of God? When did it come?

1. **Old Testament Predictions of the Kingdom** (The height of Israel's glory was under the kingship of David approximately 1,000 B.C.)
   - A. **Isaiah 2:1-4 (750 B.C.)**
     1. Last days
     2. Mountains (Symbolizes kingdoms): Mountain of the Lord, chief of the mountains
     3. All nations
     4. Jerusalem
   - B. **Daniel 2:31-45 (550 B.C.)**
     1. Daniel interprets King Nebuchadnezzar's dream
     2. Empires
     3. Babylonian: gold
     4. Medo-Persian: silver
     5. Alexander the Great: bronze
     6. Roman: iron (iron and clay)
   - C. Rock – cut out not by human hands (therefore God)
   - D. Rock becomes huge mountain
     1. Filled the whole earth – the vision for world evangelism
     2. Kingdom that will never be destroyed (v. 44)

2. **New Testament Predictions of the Kingdom** (Traditional Dates)
   - A. John the Baptist (**25 A.D.**)
     1. Kingdom is near (**Matthew 3:1-6**)
   - B. Jesus (**30 A.D.**)
     1. Kingdom is near (**Matthew 4:17**)
     2. Kingdom will come in the lifetime of some of the disciples (**Mark 9:1**)
     3. Kingdom will come with power (**Mark 9:1**)
     4. Kingdom entered by new birth (**John 3:1-7**)
     5. Kingdom is within you (**Luke 17:20-21**)

6. Peter is given the keys (**Matthew 16:13-19**). Church and the Kingdom are the same and will be built on the truth that Jesus is the Christ (**1 Corinthians 3:11**).

7. Joseph of Arimathea was still waiting for the Kingdom when Jesus died (**Luke 23:50-51**).

8. Repentance and forgiveness of sins will be preached first in Jerusalem to all nations (**Luke 24:44-49**).

3. Fulfillment of the Old and New Testament Predictions Acts 1-2 (33 A.D.)

   A. Last days (**Acts 2:17**)
      1. Isaiah 2:2
   B. All nations (**Acts 2:5**)
      1. Isaiah 2:2
      2. Luke 24:47
   C. Jerusalem (**Acts 2:5**)
      1. Isaiah 2:3
      2. Luke 24:44-49
   D. Eternal Kingdom (**Acts 2:37-42**)
      1. Daniel 2:31-45
   E. Date of coming approximately **33 A.D.** (**Acts 1-2**)
      1. Old Testament prophecy
      2. John the Baptist "is near" (**Matthew 3:1-2**)
      3. Jesus – "is near" (**Matthew 4:17**)
   F. Lifetime (**Acts 2:14**)
      1. Mark 9:1
      2. "Some" – Judas died (**Acts 1:18-19**)
   G. Power (**Acts 1:8, Acts 2:1-4**)
      1. Mark 9:1
   H. New birth (**Acts 2:38**)
      1. Water and Spirit (**John 3:1-7**)
   I. Kingdom within (**Acts 2:37-38**)
      1. Luke 17:20 - 21
   J. Peter with the keys (**Acts 2:14, 38**)
      1. Matthew 16:19
   K. Repentance and forgiveness of sin (**Acts 2:38**)

1. **Luke 24:44-49**
4. **Conclusion**
   A. The church is the Kingdom of God on earth established in approximately **33 A.D.**
   B. **Acts 2:42** As citizens of the Kingdom and members of the body (the church), we must be devoted to doctrine, to the fellowship, to the breaking of bread, and to prayer.
   C. **Matthew 6:33** We must seek His Kingdom first. Ask them to commit themselves to at least Sunday Services and Midweek Services.

LIGHT AND DARKNESS

Introduction: 1 Peter 2:9-10

Darkness	Light
Not a People of God	People of God
No Mercy	Mercy
Lost	Saved
Not a Christian	Christian
Not a Disciple	Disciple

A. Every person is either in the darkness or the light. There is no twilight zone.

B. Where are you?

1. Darkness
   A. Isaiah 59:1-2
      1. Sin separates us from God.

WALL

DARKNESS MAN		LIGHT GOD

SIN

      2. For a man to have a relationship with God, the wall must be broken down – sin must be forgiven.
      3. The point in time sin is forgiven is the point in time a person is saved.

B. Romans 3:23-25
  1. Who has sinned? Everyone!

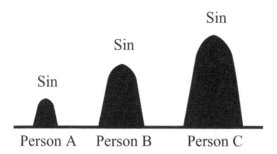

Sin

Sin

Sin

Person A   Person B   Person C

  2. Who is further away from God, a person who sins a little or a person who sins a lot? All are equal, all are lost. Therefore, a good moral life does not save you. You cannot earn your salvation by your good deeds.
  3. Faith in the blood of Jesus saves you (v. 25).

C. What is Sin?
  1. Galatians 5:19-21 (sins of commission)
  2. 2 Timothy 3:1-5 (sins of commission)
  3. James 4:17 (sins of omission)

D. What is the eternal consequence of sin? **Romans 6:23**

WAGES OF SIN	GIFT OF GOD
Death	Eternal Life
Hell	Heaven
Darkness	Light

22

2. **Light**
   A. **John 3:1-7** Born again (v. 3), born of water and Spirit (v. 5), born again (v. 7).

   B. This must be a personal decision as an adult.

   C. What message must one believe to be in the light? To be saved? **Acts 2:22-24.**
      1. Jesus is from God (v. 22).
      2. Jesus raised physically from the dead (v. 24).
      3. Everyone is responsible for the crucifixion of Christ (v. 23). All have sinned (**Romans 3:23**).

   D. Response of people **Acts 2:37**
      1. Cut to the heart.
      2. What shall we do?

   E. Once the people believed, what did they do? **Acts 2:38-42**
      1. "Repent" (Greek = to turn)
      2. "Baptized" (Greek = to be immersed)
         a. Sin forgiven. Therefore, this is the point in time a person is saved.
         b. The Holy Spirit was given to each who responded. Therefore, each new disciple received power to live as God commands.

F. Romans 6:1-4

Baptism is the sharing (a participation) in the death, burial and resurrection of Christ. (More than just a symbol.)

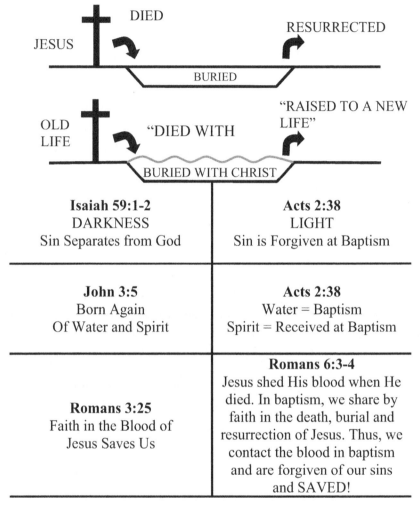

Isaiah 59:1-2 DARKNESS Sin Separates from God	**Acts 2:38** LIGHT Sin is Forgiven at Baptism
John 3:5 Born Again Of Water and Spirit	**Acts 2:38** Water = Baptism Spirit = Received at Baptism
Romans 3:25 Faith in the Blood of Jesus Saves Us	**Romans 6:3-4** Jesus shed His blood when He died. In baptism, we share by faith in the death, burial and resurrection of Jesus. Thus, we contact the blood in baptism and are forgiven of our sins and SAVED!

3. **Traditions/False Doctrines – Matthew 15:6-9**
   A. Infant Baptism
   1. Personal faith is needed (**Colossians 2:12**).
   2. Began approximately third century A.D.
   3. Original sin

24

a. **Ezekiel 18:20**
　　　b. Became "church doctrine" in 549 A.D.
　B. Praying Jesus into your heart
　　　1. Revelation 3:20 This passage is taken out of
　　　　context. This verse is addressed to Christians.
　　　2. Began in the early 1800's in America.

4. Sinful nature
　Suggest to the individual with whom you are studying that he
　or she write out and be specific about various sins they have
　committed during their life. This is so that they might see the
　gravity and magnitude of their sin. This is confidential and
　should only be shared with those who are studying with the
　person.

NEW TESTAMENT CONVERSION

1. **The Major Conversions in Acts**
   A. **Conversions**
      1. **Acts 2:36-47** First Christians in Jerusalem
      2. **Acts 8:26-39** Ethiopian Eunuch
      3. **Acts 16:22-34** Philippian jailer and his family
      4. **Acts 9:1-22** Paul
         Acts 22:3-16 Paul
      5. **Acts 18:24-26** Apollos
      6. **Acts 19:1-5** Ephesians

   B. **Questions concerning Conversions**
      (Use above Conversions 1 – 4 only)
      A. What was preached?
      B. What was the person's (people's) response to the message?
      C. How long did the person (people) take to make the decision?
      D. What was their response after baptism?

2. **Refuting False Doctrines**
   A. "Pray Jesus into your heart:" This phrase is never mentioned in the Bible. People may use **Revelation 3:20** about Jesus knocking at the door, however, you must examine this Scripture in context. This Scripture does not teach how to become a Christian and be saved, but how to come back to God after becoming lukewarm. It is addressed to disciples who already responded to Christ in faith, repentance and baptism.

   "Accept Jesus into your heart:" This is the same teaching as "praying Jesus into your heart" – just different terminology. Usually based on **Romans 10:9**. Again, you must look at Scripture in context. Paul is addressing the problem of the Israelites: Unbelief that Jesus was the Christ, the Son of God. Read further on to **Romans 10:13**. When do you call on the name of the Lord? At baptism (**Acts 22:16**).

B. Infant baptism: A baby cannot have faith, and since we are baptized through faith in the power of God (**Colossians 2:12**), babies cannot be baptized.

Original sin: **Ezekiel 18:20** teaches there is no original sin; each person is responsible for his own actions and will be judged accordingly. Therefore, babies are born sinless and will be saved if they die.

C. "Baptism does not save you:" **1 Peter 3:21** states that baptism does save you through the resurrection of Jesus Christ. **Acts 2:38** teaches that sin is forgiven at baptism – one is saved at the point sin is forgiven.

D. "Baptism is a work – yet we are saved by faith" (**Ephesians 2:8**): **Colossians 2:12** teaches that we are saved by faith in the working of God at baptism.

E. "Baptism is an outward sign of an inward grace:" **Romans 6:2-4** states that baptism is an actual participation in the death, burial and resurrection of Christ. It is not merely a sign or symbol.

F. "Baptism is not important, after all, look at what Paul said in **1 Corinthians 1:17**:" Paul does not diminish the importance of baptism here. (Paul himself was baptized to have his sins forgiven in **Acts 22:16**.) In context (read **1 Corinthians 1:10-17**), Paul makes the point that he does not want people following men (denominationalism). He mentions baptism several times in the passage.

G. "The thief on the cross was not baptized and Jesus told him that they would see each other in Paradise:" Jesus had not even died yet, and baptism is participating in his death, burial and resurrection (**Romans 6:2-4**). Also, on earth, Jesus had the power to forgive sins (**Matthew 9:2-6**).

H. "Believers baptism:" This is baptism as an adult, but it is not done in conjunction with the understanding that one is being saved at this point in time (**John 3:5; Acts 2:38**). "Retroactive understanding" is not sufficient for salvation.

THE CROSS

1. **Passion Account**
   Read **Matthew 26:31 - 28:10**
   Suggested Reading Intervals:
   **26:31-35   27:27-31
   26:36-46   27:32-44
   26:47-56   27:45-56
   26:57-68   27:57-61
   26:69-75   27:62-66
   27:1-10   28:1-10
   27:11-26**

2. **Physical Death**
   Read the medical account of Jesus' physical death.

3. **Personal Responsibility**
   A. Remember there were many others who died by crucifixion in the first century. It was not the fact that Jesus was painfully crucified that makes Him unique; it was that He was crucified for you, in your place. He died on the cross for you.
   B. **Romans 3:23**
   C. **Isaiah 59:1-2**
   D. **Matthew 27:46** Jesus was separated from God by your sins.
   E. Share the sins that you committed before being baptized and your feelings of being forgiven at baptism. Ask the person with whom you are studying to share and confess their sins.
   F. **Isaiah 53:4-6** Substitute your name.
   G. Watch either *The Passion Of The Christ* (Gibson) or *The Cross* (KNN Productions) and afterward discuss Christ's ultimate sacrifice demonstrating God's incredible grace.

The Medical Account of the Crucifixion of Christ
A Physician Analyzes The Crucifixion
by Dr. C. Truman Davis

About a decade ago, reading Jim Bishop's *The Day Christ Died*, I realized that I had for years taken the crucifixion more or less for granted – that I had grown callous to its horror by a too easy familiarity with the grim details and a too distant friendship with our Lord. It finally occurred to me that, though a physician, I did not even know the actual immediate cause of death. The Gospel writers do not help us much on this point, because crucifixion and scourging were so common during their lifetime that they apparently considered a detailed description unnecessary. So, we have only the concise words of the Evangelists: "Pilate, having scourged Jesus, delivered Him to them to be crucified – and they crucified Him."

I have no competence to discuss the infinite psychic and spiritual sufferings of the Incarnate God atoning for the sins of fallen man. But it seemed to me that as a physician I might pursue the physiological and anatomical aspects of our Lord's passion at some detail. What did the body of Jesus of Nazareth actually endure during those hours of torture?

This led me first to a study of the practice of crucifixion itself; that is, torture and execution by fixation to a cross. Apparently, the first known practice of crucifixion was by the Persians. Alexander and his generals brought it back to the Mediterranean world – to Egypt and to Carthage. The Romans apparently learned the practice from the Carthaginians and (as with almost everything the Romans did) rapidly developed a very high degree of efficiency and skill at it. A number of Roman authors (Livy, Cicero, Tacitus) comment on crucifixion, and several innovations, modifications and variations are described in the ancient literature.

For instance, the upright portion of the cross (or stipes) could have the cross-arm (or patibulum) attached two or three feet below its top in what we commonly think of as the Latin cross. The most common form used in our Lord's day, however, was the Tau cross, shaped like our T. In this cross, the patibulum was placed in a notch at the top of the stipes. There is archeological evidence that it was on this type of cross that Jesus was crucified.

Without any historical or Biblical proof, Medieval and Renaissance painters have given us our picture of Christ carrying the entire cross. But the upright post, or stipes, was generally fixed permanently in the ground at the site of execution and the condemned man was forced to carry the patibulum, weighing about 110 pounds, from the prison to the place of execution.

Many of the painters and most of the sculptors of crucifixion, also show the nails through the palms. Historical Roman accounts and experimental work have established that the nails were driven between the small bones of the wrists (radial and ulna) and not through the palms. Nails driven through the palms will strip out between the fingers when made to support the weight of the human body. The misconception may have come about through a misunderstanding of Jesus' words to Thomas, "Observe my hands." Anatomists, both modern and ancient, have always considered the wrist as part of the hand.

A titulus, or small sign, stating the victim's crime was usually placed on a staff, carried at the front of the procession from the prison, and later nailed to the cross so that it extended above the head. This sign with its staff nailed to the top of the cross would have given it somewhat the characteristic form of the Latin cross.

But, of course, the physical passion of the Christ began in Gethsemane. Of the many aspects of this initial suffering, the one of greatest physiological interest is the bloody sweat. It is interesting that St. Luke, the physician, is the only one to mention this. He says, "And being in agony, He prayed the longer. And His sweat became as drops of blood, trickling down upon the ground."

Every ruse (ploy) imaginable has been used by modern scholars to explain away this description, apparently under the mistaken impression that this just does not happen. A great deal of effort could have been saved had the doubters consulted the medical literature. Though very rare, the phenomenon of Hematidrosis, or bloody sweat, is well documented. Under great emotional stress of the kind our Lord suffered, tiny capillaries in the sweat glands can break, thus mixing blood with sweat. This process might well have produced marked weakness and possible shock.

After the arrest in the middle of the night, Jesus was next brought before the Sanhedrin and Caiaphas, the High Priest; it is here that the first

30

physical trauma was inflicted. A soldier struck Jesus across the face for remaining silent when questioned by Caiaphas. The palace guards then blind-folded Him and mockingly taunted Him to identify them as they each passed by, spat upon Him, and struck Him in the face.

In the early morning, battered and bruised, dehydrated and exhausted from a sleepless night, Jesus is taken across the Praetorium of the Fortress Antonia, the seat of government of the Procurator of Judea, Pontius Pilate. You are, of course, familiar with Pilate's action in attempting to pass responsibility to Herod Antipas, the Tetrarch of Judea. Jesus apparently suffered no physical mistreatment at the hands of Herod and was returned to Pilate. It was then, in response to the cries of the mob, that Pilate ordered Bar-Abbas released and condemned Jesus to scourging and crucifixion.

There is much disagreement among authorities about the unusual scourging as a prelude to crucifixion. Most Roman writers from this period do not associate the two. Many scholars believe that Pilate originally ordered Jesus scourged as his full punishment and that the death sentence by crucifixion came only in response to the taunt by the mob that the Procurator was not properly defending Caesar against this pretender who allegedly claimed to be the King of the Jews.

Preparations for the scourging were carried out when the Prisoner was stripped of His clothing and His hands tied to a post above His head. It is doubtful the Romans would have made any attempt to follow the Jewish Law in this matter, but the Jews had an ancient law prohibiting more than forty lashes.

The Roman legionnaire steps forward with the flagrum (or flagellum) in his hand. This is a short whip consisting of several heavy, leather thongs with two small balls of lead attached near the ends of each. The heavy whip is brought down with full force again and again across Jesus' shoulders, back and legs. At first the thongs cut through the skin only. Then, as the blows continue, they cut deeper into the subcutaneous tissues, producing first an oozing of blood from the capillaries and veins of the skin, and finally spurting arterial bleeding from vessels in the underlying muscles.

The small balls of lead first produce large, deep bruises which are broken open by subsequent blows. Finally, the skin of the back is hanging in long ribbons and the entire area is an unrecognizable mass of torn,

31

bleeding tissue. When it is determined by the centurion in charge that the prisoner is near death, the beating is finally stopped.

The half-fainting Jesus is then untied and allowed to slump to the stone pavement, wet with His own blood. The Roman soldiers see a great joke in this provincial Jew claiming to be king. They throw a robe across His shoulders and place a stick in His hand for a scepter. They still need a crown to make their travesty complete. Flexible branches covered with long thorns (commonly used in bundles for firewood) are plaited into the shape of a crown and this is pressed into His scalp. Again, there is copious bleeding, the scalp being one of the most vascular areas of the body.

After mocking Him and striking Him across the face, the soldiers take the stick from His hand and strike Him across the head, driving the thorns deeper into His scalp. Finally, they tire of their sadistic sport and the robe is torn from His back. Already having adhered to the clots of blood and serum in the wounds, its removal causes excruciating pain just as in the careless removal of a surgical bandage, and almost as though He were again being whipped, the wounds once more begin to bleed.

In deference to Jewish custom, the Romans return His garments. The heavy patibulum of the cross is tied across His shoulders, and the procession of the condemned Christ, two thieves, and the execution detail of Roman soldiers headed by a centurion begins its slow journey along the Via Dolorosa. In spite of His efforts to walk erect, the weight of the heavy wooden beam, together with the shock produced by copious blood loss, is too much. He stumbles and falls. The rough wood of the beam gouges into the lacerated skin and muscles of the shoulders. He tries to rise, but human muscles have been pushed beyond their endurance.

The centurion, anxious to get on with the crucifixion, selects a stalwart North African onlooker, Simon of Cyrene, to carry the cross. Jesus follows, still bleeding and sweating the cold, clammy sweat of shock, until the 650-yard journey from the fortress Antonia to Golgotha is finally completed.

Jesus is offered wine mixed with myrrh, a mild analgesic mixture. He refuses to drink. Simon is ordered to place the patibulum on the ground and Jesus is quickly thrown backward with His shoulders against the wood. The legionnaire feels for the depression at the front of the wrist.

He drives a heavy, square, wrought-iron nail through the wrist and deep into the wood. Quickly, he moves to the other side and repeats the action being careful not to pull the arms too tightly, but to allow some flexion and movement. The patibulum is then lifted in place at the top of the stipes and the titulus reading "Jesus of Nazareth, King of the Jews" is nailed in place.

The left foot is now pressed backward against the right foot, and with both feet extended, toes down, a nail is driven through the arch of each, leaving the knees moderately flexed. The Victim is now crucified. As He slowly sags down with more weight on the nails in the wrists excruciating pain shoots along the fingers and up the arms to explode in the brain – the nails in the writs are putting pressure on the median nerves. As He pushes Himself upward to avoid this stretching torment, He places His full weight on the nail through His feet. Again, there is the searing agony of the nail tearing through the nerves between the metatarsal bones of the feet.

At this point, as the arms fatigue, great waves of cramps sweep over the muscles, knotting them in deep, relentless, throbbing pain. With these cramps comes the inability to push Himself upward. Hanging by his arms, the pectoral muscles are paralyzed, and the intercostal muscles are unable to act. Air can be drawn into the lungs but cannot be exhaled. Jesus fights to raise Himself in order to get even one short breath. Finally, carbon dioxide builds up in the lungs and in the blood stream and the cramps partially subside. Spasmodically, he is able to push Himself upward to exhale and bring in the life-giving oxygen. It was undoubtedly during these periods that He uttered the seven short sentences recorded:

The first, looking down at the Roman soldiers throwing dice for His seamless garment, "Father, forgive them for they know not what they do."

The second, to the penitent thief, "Today thou shalt be with me in Paradise."

The third, looking down at the terrified, grief-stricken adolescent John – the beloved Apostle – he said, "Behold thy mother." Then, looking to His mother Mary, "Woman behold thy son."

The fourth cry is from the beginning of the 22nd Psalm, "My God, my God, why has thou forsaken me?"

There are hours of limitless pain, cycles of twisting, joint-rending cramps, intermittent partial asphyxiation, searing pain where tissue is torn from His lacerated back as He moves up and down against the rough timber. Then another

agony begins... A terrible crushing pain deep in the chest as the pericardium slowly fills with serum and begins to compress the heart.

One remembers again the 22nd Psalm, the 14th verse: "I am poured out like water, and all my bones are out of joint; my heart is like wax; it is melted in the midst of my bowels."

It is now almost over. The loss of tissue fluids has reached a critical level; the compressed heart is struggling to pump heavy, thick, sluggish blood into the tissue; the tortured lungs are making a frantic effort to gasp in small gulps of air. The markedly dehydrated tissues send their flood of stimuli to the brain.

Jesus gasps His fifth cry, "I thirst."

One remembers another verse from the prophetic 22nd Psalm: "My strength is dried up like a potsherd; and my tongue cleaveth to my jaws; and thou has brought me into the dust of death."

A sponge soaked in posca, the cheap, sour wine – which is the staple drink of the Roman legionaries – is lifted to His lips. He apparently does not take any of the liquid. The body of Jesus is now in extremis, and He can feel the chill of death creeping through His tissues. This realization brings out His sixth words, possibly little more than a tortured whisper, "It is finished." His mission of atonement has completed. Finally, He can allow his body to die.

With one last surge of strength, he once again presses His torn feet against the nail, straightens His legs, takes a deeper breath, and utters His seventh and last cry, "Father! Into thy hands I commit my spirit."

The rest you know. In order that the Sabbath not be profaned, the Jews asked that the condemned men be dispatched and removed from the crosses. The common method of ending a crucifixion was by crucifracture, the breaking of the bones of the legs. This prevented the victim from pushing himself upward; thus, the tension could not be relieved from the muscles of the chest and rapid suffocation occurred.

34

The legs of the two thieves were broken, but when the soldiers came to Jesus, they saw that this was unnecessary.

Apparently to make doubly sure of death, the legionnaire drove his lance through the fifth interspace between the ribs, upward through the pericardium and into the heart. The 34th verse of the 19th chapter of the Gospel according to St. John reports, "And immediately there came out blood and water." That is, there was an escape of water fluid from the sac surrounding the heart, giving postmortem evidence that our Lord died not the usual crucifixion death by suffocation, but of heart failure due to shock and constriction of the heart by fluid in the pericardium.

Thus, we have had our glimpse – including the medical evidence – of that epitome of evil which man has exhibited toward man and toward God. It has been a terrible sight, and more than enough to leave us despondent and depressed. How grateful we can be that we have the great sequel in the infinite mercy of God toward man – at once the miracle of the atonement and the expectation of the triumphant Easter morning.

From *New Wine Magazine, April 1982*. Originally published in *Arizona Medicine, March 1965*, Arizona Medical Association.

BAPTISM WITH
THE HOLY SPIRIT

Introduction: Jesus was given the Spirit in full measure, no limit (**John 3:34**). There are three measures of the Holy Spirit:

1. **The Indwelling of the Holy Spirit**
   A. Received at baptism (**Acts 2:38**)

2. **The Baptism with the Holy Spirit**
   A. Characteristics in **Acts 2** and **Acts 10**
      1. Promise (not command), **Acts 1:4-5**
      2. Predicted (prophesied)
      3. Came without warning. (People were not specifically praying for it.)
      4. Languages
      5. Purpose: To usher in the Kingdom with power

   B. Accounts of the Baptism with the Holy Spirit
      1. To the Jews – in Jerusalem (**Acts 2**)
      2. To the Gentiles – begins with Cornelius (**Acts 10**)
         a. Note: Cornelius and his household were water baptized in v. 48, and saved at baptism.
         b. Peter explained actions to the Jews (**Acts 11:1-18**).
         c. "At the beginning" referring to Jerusalem (**Acts 11:15**)
         d. "The message" will save (Acts 11:14), yet the Baptism of the Holy Spirit came before Peter finished preaching. (Acts 10:44)

   C. Does the Baptism with the Holy Spirit still exist today? **Ephesians 4:4-6**: There is "one baptism," but which one? (Written about 60-62 A.D.) There are three baptism options:

1. John's baptism passed when new covenant began (**Acts 19:1-5**).
2. The Baptism with the Holy Spirit (**Acts 2 and 10**) is no longer present as it was a prophecy/promise that has been fulfilled. It was never a general command for all Christians.
3. Baptism with water in the name of Jesus Christ for the forgiveness of sins to receive the indwelling of the Holy Spirit.
   a. Jesus commanded this baptism (**Matthew 28:18-20**).
   b. This baptism is recorded all the way through the Book of Acts and the Epistles. **1 Peter 3:21** (written around 64 A.D.) makes reference to this water baptism of salvation.
   c. It had to be the "one baptism" of **Ephesians 4:4-6,** as it was the only one practiced by 60-62 A.D. when Ephesians was written.

3. The Miraculous Gifts of the Holy Spirit (next lesson)
   A. Received by the Apostles' laying on of hands
   B. No longer present today

THE MIRACULOUS GIFTS OF THE HOLY SPIRIT

1. **Types of Miraculous Gifts**
   A. **1 Corinthians 12:8-10**
      1. Wisdom
      2. Knowledge
      3. Faith
      4. Healing
      5. Miracles
      6. Prophecy
      7. Distinguishing Spirits
      8. Tongues
      9. Interpretation of Tongues
   B. **Mark 16:16-18** Some will be able to:
      1. Drink poison and not die
      2. Be bitten by snakes and not die (**Acts 28:5**)

2. **Types of "Laying on of Hands"**
   A. **Blessing (Acts 13:3)**
   B. **Healing**
      1. Ananias heals Paul's blindness (**Acts 9:17-18**).
      2. Paul heals Publius' father on Malta (**Acts 28:8**).
   C. **Passing on the Gifts**
      3. Apostles would pass on the gifts (**Acts 8:18**).
      4. These people could not pass on the gifts they received.
         a. **Acts 6:1-8**: Context is the choosing of "The Seven." This is the first occasion that the gifts were passed. Stephen immediately starts to perform miraculous signs among the people with God's power (v. 8).

b. **Acts 8:1-25**: Context is after Stephen's martyrdom. Great persecution breaks out. Most leave, but the Apostles stay in Jerusalem. Philip, one of The Seven who had received the gifts in **Acts 6:1-8**, goes to Samaria. He performs many miraculous signs and healings to get people to believe (v. 12), including Simon the Sorcerer (v. 13) and they are baptized. (They became Christians and thus receive the forgiveness of sins and the gift (indwelling) of the Holy Spirit as promised in **Acts 2:38**.) When the Apostles come to Samaria, Simon saw the Spirit's gifts were only given by Apostles' laying on of hands and offers them money for the ability (**Acts 8:18**). Note: Simon did not ask Philip for the gifts, because he never saw Philip pass them on. In fact, he could not. Simon is rebuked for having the wrong motivation.

c. **Acts 19:1-6**: Paul finds disciples in Ephesus who did not know what the Holy Spirit was because they had only received John's baptism. Then they were baptized into the name of Jesus Christ to receive the indwelling of the Holy Spirit (v.5). Then they receive the miraculous gifts of prophecy and speaking in tongues by the laying on of Paul's hands (v.6). Paul is an Apostle.

3. General Observations

A. Apostles were able to pass on the gifts because they were Apostles. The Apostles possessed the ability to perform miracles even during the ministry of Christ (**Luke 9:1**). The ability to perform the gifts were not given at Pentecost.

B. **1 Corinthians 12 and 14** are not the "directives" on how to receive tongues (the church there had already received them), but rather the "correctives" on how to use them because everyone was speaking at the same time and misusing this amazing gift. **1 Corinthians 12:28-30** shows that tongues as a gift were not given to everyone in the church. Thus, the

39

concept of a "Pentecostal church" (every member speaking in tongues) is against Scripture.

C. **1 Corinthians 13:8-10** "Perfection" here could not mean the coming of Christ because it is in the neuter gender in Greek, not the masculine gender. When perfection comes probably refers to the canonization of the Bible sometime after the first century. At that time, all the miraculous gifts would be gone because all the Apostles and those to whom they passed the gifts would have died.

D. The two purposes of the miraculous gifts from **1 Corinthians 14:20-22** was: 1) To get non-believers to believe, and 2) To edify the Christians and strengthen their faith. **Note:** Tongues were ONLY to be used to bring non-believers to faith

E. Now the Bible fulfills these needs. Thus, the church today does not need apostles or miraculous gifts.

F. **2 Thessalonians 2:9-10** shows there can be miracles by Satan today. Satan's purpose is to deceive people about the truth, so they will not be saved.

G. Speaking in "tongues" is common in many religions (Mormon, Catholic, Islam, etc.) because religion often becomes dried and staid. These are also called "ecstatic utterances" – non-understandable sounds and fragments of speech.

H. A person can be filled with the Spirit without speaking in tongues (**Ephesians 5:18-19**).

I. Jesus never spoke in tongues and He was accorded the full-measure of the Spirit (**John 3:34-36**).

THE CHURCH

1. **Colossians 1:15-18**
   A. The church is the body of Christ.
   B. The body needs the head.
   C. The church is essential to Christianity.

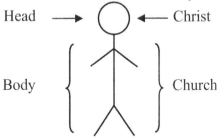

2. **Ephesians 2:19-21**
   A. The church is the family of God.

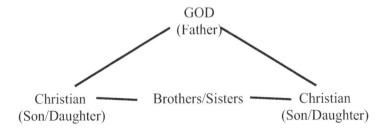

   B. **1 Corinthians 12:12-13** teaches we are baptized into the body of Christ, the church.

   C. **Romans 6:3-4** teaches we are also baptized into Christ. Baptism is when we become a Christian, a son of God, and at this same point, we become members of the church – the family of God.

41

3. **Ephesians 2:20**
   Cornerstone: Christ
   Foundation: Apostles and Prophets
    Apostles = New Testament Bible
    Prophets = Old Testament
    The church is based on the Word of God only.
4. Have you ever wondered why there are so many denominations?
   (1,200 or more exist in the U.S. alone.)
   A. The Bible teaches there is one church.
    1. Ephesians 4:4-6 – One Body
    2. Romans 12:4-5 – One Body
    3. 1 Corinthians 12:12-13 – One Body

   B. Divisions in Christendom may be of Satan or of God.
    1. 1 Corinthians 1:10-13 Division is sin, when following personalities and in time their writings (traditions of men that contradict the Word – false doctrines). **Matthew 15:6-9**
    2. Luke 12:51-53; John 10:19-21 Division will occur and is righteous, when an individual, church or movement aligns themselves with the Word of God. The Jews considered themselves "God's people," yet Jesus' words (the truth) divided them into two groups – those who opposed Him and those who obeyed Him.

   C. The following are the major historical divisions in Christendom – some were formed by a noble stand for the truth (though not a complete return), while others were departures from the truth.

    1. Through the centuries the church was corrupted by traditions of men – false doctrines, such as: infant baptism, original sin, perpetual virginity of Mary, priests as clergy, papal infallibility, etc. This becomes the **Catholic Church**. In 364 AD the Roman Empire is split into two parts. This division leads to a split in Christianity – the eastern portion becomes the **Eastern**

42

Orthodox Church and the western section becomes the **Roman Catholic Church**. Practices diverge. For example: The Orthodox Church has married priests, while Roman Catholic priests are celibate. The "Great Schism" occurs in 1054 AD, as the leaders of "each church" excommunicate each other.

2. **1500's Reformation Movement** – Martin Luther (Lutheran Church) takes a stand against the Roman Catholic Church on these convictions: Bible authority over church authority, salvation by faith not works, and the priesthood of all believers, yet still baptizes infants. Other noted reformers were John Calvin (Presbyterian Church), and Ulrich Zwingli (Reformed Church), as well as Conrad Grebel (Anabaptists). The Anabaptists were heavily persecuted by Catholics and by some reformers, because of their stand for adult baptism. Henry VIII (Anglican Church / Church of England) broke from the Catholic Church over his right to divorce his wife. He appoints himself head of the church. Later in the United States, the Anglican Church becomes the Episcopalian Church, since members will not follow the king of England.

3. **1700's Great Awakening Movement** – John and Charles Wesley (Methodist Church) divide from Church of England over: Personal transforming decision for Christ not state religion, high accountability of members, and preaching to the "unchurched;" but continued to practice infant baptism.

4. **1800's Restoration Movement** – Alexander Campbell and Barton Stone (Mainline Church of Christ and Conservative Christian Church) Take a stand against both Catholic and Protestant doctrines of salvation. They preached that to be saved one must have personal faith in Christ, repentance and baptism (immersion) for the forgiveness of sin to receive the Holy Spirit. In reaction to Catholicism, their congregations are

43

autonomous – self-governing. (In 1906 was the formal split between Mainline Church of Christ, which is non-instrumental, and the Conservative Christian Church, which is instrumental.) Joseph Smith (Mormon Church) divides from Restoration Movement in 1830 over his "new revelation" – the Book of Mormon.

5. **1967 Crossroads Movement (Total Commitment Movement)** was initiated by Chuck Lucas. Controversial, though never departing from the Mainline Church of Christ, the Crossroads Church near the University of Florida pioneers evangelizing the secular campuses of United States, "counting the cost" with each person that desires to be baptized, and the shepherding of new converts.

6. **1979 Boston Movement (International Church of Christ)** was formed by Kip McKean. He was baptized at the University of Florida in 1972. In time, the Boston Movement divided from not only the Mainline Churches of Christ, but also the Crossroads Movement over the Bible's Five Core Convictions: 1) Bible Church not just New Testament Church **(2 Timothy 3:16-17)**; 2) Speak where the Bible is silent and be silent where the Bible speaks; in other words, we are "free" to practice and name anything as long as it does not conflict with Scripture **(Genesis 2:19)**; 3) Only baptized disciples are true Christians, members of God's church, and should be in discipling relationships **(Matthew 28:19-20)**. 4) God's plan is for a central leadership of His people, as autonomy for a local congregation is sin **(Numbers 27:12-18)**. 5) God's will is for the evangelization of the nations in this generation **(1 Timothy 2:3-4)**. In 2002, the International Churches of Christ returned to Mainline Church of Christ theology. Of note: Each congregation became autonomous (self-governing), discipling called "optional," central leadership was labeled "unbiblical," and the vision for the evangelization of the nations in this

44

generation "impossible." Around the world, thousands fall-away.

7. **2006 SoldOut Movement (Portland Movement / International Christian Church)** officially begins in Portland, Oregon based on the Bible's Five Core Convictions preached again by Kip McKean. It began as a revival movement within what was left of the International Churches of Christ. The International Churches of Christ separated from the International Christian Churches, because of the SoldOut Movement's stand on the Bible's Five Core Convictions.

5. What is the "one church?"
   A. **Acts 11:25-26 Church = Disciples = Christians** When God looks down from Heaven, He sees one church – all the baptized disciples around the world, who are "sold-out" in obeying His Word. This is called the "church universal" – the one true church (Ephesians 4:4-6).
   B. A local congregation is called the "visible church." In the first century, all the "visible churches" made up the "church universal." However, since so many "visible churches" have departed from true doctrine and because all sold-out baptized disciples are not in one fellowship, we should strive to be a member of a local congregation where everyone is sold-out and under central leadership.
   C. The Greek word for church is "ekklesia" which means "assembly" or "called out." ("Ek" meaning "out" and "kaleo" meaning "to call.") To be a disciple is to be "called out" from the world. Therefore, the church in the Bible was the "assembly" of the "called out."
   D. There are several names in the Bible for God's Church: Disciples, Christians, Church of God, Church of Christ, The Way, Church of the Firstborn, Saints, etc... Since we are free to choose any name for our fellowship and our

45

fellowship goes around the world, we call ourselves the "International Christian Church."

6. **1 Corinthians 12:14-27**
   A. We need the body. The body needs us (v. 21).
   B. Be involved on a "relationship level" in the church (v. 26).

7. **Hebrews 10:23-25**
   A. Do not miss church.

   B. The fellowship helps us to be unswerving in our commitment (v. 23).

   C. Another purpose of fellowship is to encourage each other so we will remain faithful (v. 24).

   D. A disciple will joyfully come to all meeting of the body: i.e. Sunday and Midweek Services, Devotionals, Jubilees, Retreats, Seminars, etc. Begin to rearrange your schedule to come to all the meetings of the body.

8. **Contribution**
   A. **Malachi 3:6-12** Do not rob God by not giving your offerings. On Sundays, we give to meet the local ministry needs. Benevolent offerings are given at Midweek Services. Annual Missions Contributions support the planting of new churches, as well as the ongoing support for third world congregations.

   B. **2 Corinthians 9:6-8** Giving should be from a "cheerful heart" – not under compulsion. God blesses you when you generously sacrifice.

THE STUDY OF THE BOOK OF ACTS

Chapters 1-8
BUILDING A GREAT CHURCH

Chapters 9-15
FORCEFULLY ADVANCING THE KINGDOM

Chapters 16-21
TURNING THE WORLD UPSIDEDOWN

Chapters 22-28
THE EVANGELIZATION OF THE NATIONS IN A GENERATION

FOLLOW UP STUDY #1
AFTER BAPTISM, NOW WHAT?

Introduction

    A. Discuss the new disciple's first few days as a Christian.

    B. Have the new Christian share their "letter to God." If the new disciple has not had a chance to write one, encourage him/her to do so.

1. Acts 2:36-47 – The Conversion of the 3,000

    A. Discuss Biblical Conversion

        1. Review how to become a Christian.

        2. Reinforce the joy of salvation.

    B. Devoted to the Apostles' Teaching – the Word

        1. For a quiet time, suggest a book or theme – reading a chapter a day.

        2. For many, a quiet time journal is helpful.

    C. Devoted to the Fellowship

        1. Discuss the purpose of each gathering: Sunday Worship Services, Midweek Services, Devotionals, Bible Talk and Discipleship Partners.

        2. Discuss the need to initiate relationships – give not just receive.

        3. Discuss the importance of hospitality – invite people into your home for a meal.

        4. Discuss the expectation to be generous in financial sacrifices on Sundays and give a benevolent offering at the Midweek Services. Read together **2 Corinthians 9:6-11**.

    D. Devoted to Breaking Bread – Communion **(1 Corinthians 11:23-32)**

        1. Discuss purpose of the bread and the fruit of the vine.

        2. Discuss what it means to become spiritually "weak, sick and fallen asleep." How does communion prevent these conditions?

(For being spiritually sick see **Proverbs 3:12**.)

   E. Devoted to Prayer
      1. Discuss how prayer brings peace. (**Philippians 4:4-7**)
      2. Share petitions and answered prayers.

2. The Conversion of Paul (**Acts 9:18-25**)
   A. Paul immediately begins to preach.
      1. Discuss who the new disciple has shared with.
      2. Make a list of people with which to share.
   B. Paul grows powerful.
   C. Paul is persecuted.

3. **Hebrews 5:11 – 6:6 The First Principles**
   A. Strive to learn the *First Principle Studies* (elementary teachings) and go on to maturity, so you can be fruitful and not fall away.
   B. Discuss taking The First Principle Classes.

FOLLOW-UP STUDY #2
CHRIST IS YOUR LIFE

Introduction
- **A.** Discuss:
  1. Did you have daily quiet times this past week?
  2. Who did you share with and invite?
  3. Did you feel good about your level of sacrifice in time and money?
- **B.** Discuss the impact of communion on Sunday.

1. **Colossians 3:1-4**
   Raised to a New Life
   - **A.** Discuss "raised with Christ in baptism" (**Colossians 2:11-12**).
   - **B.** Discuss setting your mind (thoughts) and setting your heart (emotions) on things above.
   - **C.** Can you say, "Christ is my life?"

2. **Colossians 3:5-11**
   Put to Death
   - **A.** Be open about your greatest struggles this week.
   - **B.** Discuss practical ways to crucify these temptations and/or sins.

3. **Colossians 3:12-14**
   Put On – Clothe Yourself
   - **A.** Compassion
   - **B.** Kindness
   - **C.** Humility
   - **D.** Gentleness
   - **E.** Patience

4. **Colossians 3:15-4:1**
   New Attitudes
   - **A.** Peace (v. 15)

B. Thankful (v. 15-16)

C. Wholehearted (v. 17)

D. Family interactions (v. 18-21)

E. Employer/employee relationship (3:22, 4:1)

F. Teacher/student relationship

FOLLOW UP STUDY #3
BEST FRIENDS OF ALL TIME

Introduction

    A. Have the new Christian share about their closest relationships during their lives.

    B. Ask how close they feel to God and their spiritual family in comparison to their physical family and old friends. Ask the young Christian, "Who are your closest friends in the church?"

1. One Another Scriptures

    A. John 13:34-35 Love one another. Jesus teaches that Christians should have better relationships than people in the world. Set your mind to make Christians your best friends.

    B. Hebrews 3:12-14 Daily encouragement of one another.

    C. Ephesians 5:19-20 Worship God with one another in singing to God with psalms, hymns and spiritual songs.

    D. Colossians 1:28-29 Disciple one another. This is essential in God's plan to become mature. As we mature, we learn to instruct one another (**Romans 15:14**).

    E. Galatians 6:1-2 Gently restore one another and bear one another's burdens.

    F. James 5:16 Confess sins to one another. Discuss openness and transparency, remembering that "openness breeds openness." So, the older Christians should share their struggles first and/or their struggles as a young disciple.

    G. James 5:16-18 Pray for one another, as it makes a huge difference!

    H. Hebrews 12:14-15 Be holy and help to prevent bad attitudes ("bitter roots") in one another.

    I. 1 Thessalonians 5:12-14 Outlook toward leaders and one another.

    J. John 17:20-23 The ultimate goal of unity is world evangelism.

2. Date and Marry Only Disciples

A. 1 Corinthians 7:39 Marriage must be in the Lord

B. 2 Corinthians 6:14-18 Dating, like marriage, is a partnership where you are "yoked together." Disciples must separate from unbelievers to receive the promises of God.

C. 1 Kings 11:1-10; Nehemiah 13:23-27 Study this principle in the Old Testament. To date or marry outside of the faith is to be unfaithful to God. If you are single, have you gone on a Christian date?

D. 1 Peter 3:1-7 If you are married, are you winning your spouse? Are you going on dates with your spouse?

3. Reconcile with One Another

A. Matthew 18:15-17 Christians will sin against each other. When someone sins against you, do not gossip by going to someone else. Talk to the person who hurt you, so you can win him/her over as a friend.

B. Church discipline begins one-on-one and rarely should go to steps 2, 3 and 4.

FOLLOW UP STUDY #4
THE MISSION

Introduction
  A. Share about the visitors you most recently brought to church or Bible Talk.
  B. Ask the young disciple about their evangelism.

1. **Jesus' Mission**
   Read together:
   A. Luke 19:10
   B. Matthew 28:19-20
   C. 1 Timothy 2:3-4
      1. What was Jesus' mission?
      2. What was His vision?
      3. What is each disciple's mission?
2. **Disciples' Mission**
   A. John 15:1-16
      1. Glorifying God in **John 15** is bearing the fruit of making disciples, not simply baptizing. (**Matthew 28:19** commands us to "go and make disciples;" **John 15:16** commands us to "go and bear fruit that will last.")
      2. To bear fruit, one must be "in the vine," otherwise we will be cut off.
      3. Jesus is the perfect discipler, but He is also the perfect disciple of God **(John 15:9-10)**.
      4. To love God is to obey His commands. Discipling helps our hearts to want to obey His commands **(Matthew 28:20)**. Therefore, we must love one another by laying down our lives for each other.

   B. **The Book of Acts** records the approximate 30 years from the beginning of the church on the day of Pentecost to Paul's first incarceration in Rome. The church in the first century was a movement. Discuss the growth of those first 30 years of the first century church when all Christians were striving to be fruitful – making disciples.

1. Acts 2:41	9. Acts 11:21
2. Acts 2:47	10. Acts 12:24
3. Acts 4:4	11. Acts 13:49
4. Acts 5:14	12. Acts 14:1
5. Acts 6:1	13. Acts 14:21
6. Acts 6:7	14. Acts 16:5
7. Acts 8:4	15. Acts 17:4
8. Acts 9:31	16. Acts 28:22

17. **Acts 17:6 (RSV)** "These men who have turned the world upsidedown have come here also..."

18. **Colossians 1:6, 23** Paul wrote Colossians in 62A.D., while detained in his rented home **(Acts 28:30)**. These Scriptures attest that the known world was evangelized by 62 AD – in Paul's generation! Therefore, Jesus' vision of Matthew 28 became a reality – "the evangelization of the nations in a generation!"

C. Discuss and pray for:
1. World Evangelism
2. Mission Teams
3. Kingdom dreams... How can you use your talents for God?

FOLLOW UP STUDY #5
PERSECUTION
*THIS STUDY HAS PROVEN TO BE MOST HELPFUL
IMMEDIATELY FOLLOWING THE DISCIPLESHIP STUDY.*

Introduction – 2 Timothy 3:12 "Everyone who wants to live as a disciple will be persecuted."

1. **Jesus was persecuted.**
   A. **Family**
      1. **Mark 3:20-21** Jesus' family thought he was out of His mind. (brainwashed; mind-control)
      2. **Mark 3:31-35** Jesus prioritized His spiritual family above His physical family.
      3. **Acts 1:12-14** Though this conviction initially produced conflict, after His resurrection and ascension His mother and brothers were disciples.
   B. **Gossip and slander**
      1. **John 7:12-13** Jesus was accused of deceiving people.
      2. **John 10:19-21** The Jews – religious people – intensely persecuted Jesus through name-calling and character assassination. Jesus' teachings always divided His listeners.
   C. **Scope of persecution**
      1. **Luke 23:1-3** Jesus is condemned to a death by crucifixion through half-truths.
      2. Jesus – who was perfect – was falsely accused and misunderstood by His family and killed by religious leaders. What do you think will happen to you if you follow Jesus?

2. **The First Century Church was persecuted.**
   A. **Acts 5:17-18, 38-42**
      1. The Jewish leadership arrested the Apostles for preaching the Word, because of jealousy.

    2. Those who persecuted the Christians thought they were doing this for God, though in fact they were fighting against Him.

    3. The Apostles suffered physical mistreatment.

    4. Persecution did not stop the disciples from daily proclamation.

B. Acts 28:21-22

    1. Everywhere, the church was highly controversial.

    2. The church was called a "sect." (cult)

    3. Since the International Christian Churches have the goal of imitating Jesus and the first century church, what will happen to us? If a church is not being persecuted, what does that imply?

3. Causes of persecution. 1 Timothy 4:16 – Life and Doctrine

A. Life

    1. 1 Peter 4:3-4 The world feels condemned by those who no longer participate in its sin.

    2. 1 Peter 4:12-16 Do not be surprised or ashamed by persecution, but be sure you are persecuted for righteousness sake.

B. Doctrine

    1. Preaching the Word – **John 15:18-20; 16:1-4**

        a. Jesus warns that persecution comes to those who preach the same message as Him.

        b. Jesus warns that the price of hatred is certain, and perhaps even death.

    2. Narrow Road of Salvation – **Matthew 7:13-14**

        a. **Acts 4:12** Only an individual who believes in Jesus is saved.

        (This truth "condemns" atheists, polytheists, Jews, Muslims, Hindus, Buddhists, etc.)

        b. Disciples do not condemn the lost, they are condemned already. However, when the lost are confronted doctrinally about their condition before God, they will repent, run and/or persecute.

C. Doctrine of discipling - Matthew 28:19-20
    1. Matthew 28:19-20 Discipling, calling people to obey the Word of God, is often viewed by the world as controlling.

4. Our attitude about persecution
  A. Matthew 5:10-12
    1. Do not fear persecution. Do not care what men think about you, only God.
    2. Rejoice! You are not alone since they persecuted both Jesus and the prophets.
  B. Ephesians 6:10-18
    1. Satan is behind all persecution. Only God and His spiritual armor will give you the victory over the world.

5. Conclusion – The International Christian Churches (ICC) are a controversial Christian movement. Some call us a cult and accuse us of both brainwashing and mind-control. Many false rumors and half-truths have been spread. Newspaper articles, television shows and especially the internet have slandered the ICC, and yet, the facts are that lives have been radically changed, marriages have been healed, drug addicts have been freed, the poor have been fed and cared for, and this rapidly growing movement – the "SoldOut Movement" – is spreading around the world in this generation… Just like the first century! **(See caicc.net and usd21.org)**

Made in the USA
Las Vegas, NV
22 August 2024

94279263R00036